BLUFF YOUR WAY IN PHOTOGRAPHY

JOHN COURTIS

Ravette London

Published by Ravette Limited
3 Glenside Estate, Star Road,
Partridge Green, Horsham,
Sussex RH13 8RA
(0403) 710392

Series Editor — Anne Tauté

Cover design — Jim Wire
Typesetting — Repro-type
Printing & Binding — Cox & Wyman Ltd.
Production — Oval Projects Ltd.

The Bluffer's Guides are based on
an original ideal by Peter Wolfe.

CONTENTS

INTRODUCTION

The essence of bluff is the successful defence of an inherently weak position which, in the case of photography, implies getting good results and maintaining your image without unlimited funds or massive experience. This book is therefore about:

* holding your own against other photographers in conversation, with pointers to their feet of clay
* wearing the correct camera
* debunking myths
* knowing a bit more about other people's mistakes so that your own work looks better as a result.

It is not about:

* cinematography
* video
* adventures in the darkroom
* finding unclad models.

Getting an image on record in a form in which it reminds you, even faintly, of the scene your eye visualised is actually extremely difficult. Unless you are very skilled, it is craftier to be an informed critic than a performer. Fortunately the photographer's obsession with hardware rather than results means that there is a lot to criticise, even before you see what they produce.

Complications like developing and printing can thankfully be avoided, unless you become addicted. If you do decide to take pictures, rather than sneer knowledgeably from the sidelines, it is possible to delegate the messy bits and still give considerable pleasure to victims, relatives, friends and of course, yourself.

PROS AND AMS

There is no difficulty in distinguishing between amateurs and professionals. As in other sectors, professionals do it for the money. The fun lies in defining the different kinds of amateur so that you can impress those that are in your league, or avoid competing with those that are out of it.

1. At the one end, there is the unashamed amateur. One who is ignorant but doesn't mind showing it. This kind wants photography to be effortless and cheap.

2. Next comes the rank and file amateur, so called because he (it is nearly always a male) has almost mastered darkroom work, except for the business of cleaning up afterwards. These people therefore smell somewhat rank and anyone downwind of them can catch faint whiffs of hypo, developer and beer.

3. Then you have the experienced amateur — a dangerous breed. This lot know a great deal about the subject, and do not like being caught out.

4. The only group left is the near-professional which includes:

   a) those whose results are almost professional
   b) those whose cameras are professional.

The situation is only a little complicated by the fact that in certain respects the total professional and the total amateur come together. For example, true professionals and unashamed amateurs are wholly concerned with results. 'Did it come out properly?' is their traditional cry.

In between, the semi-professional and the experienced amateur are often distracted by their hardware, which frequently is as important as, or more important than, the results.

One useful indicator is the brown fingernail syndrome. Real pros or very dedicated amateurs wallow in black and white developer for hours, disdaining the use of rubber gloves or tongs. Do not tangle with such people, except to remind them that the noxious concoction of sulphuric acid, potassium permanganate and bleach will remove the traces.

Neither very senior professionals nor bluffers bear these marks because they delegate to professional processors. Darkrooms are to be avoided. There is nothing wrong with entering one from time to time, mainly for the atmosphere, but the idea is to be above such things. Ideally what you are trying to achieve is an image which:

a) amateurs will perceive as experienced, perhaps professional
b) professionals will feel comfortable enough with, not to dismiss you as wholly amateur.

Good reasons for not having your camera with you

a) I'm changing systems. (N.B., always 'systems' not cameras. The true enthusiast always has enough clobber to call it a system).
b) I don't like bringing the Leica/Pentax/Nikon near sea air/water/sand/children/radiation sources etc. (N.B., this argument is not valid if the audience knows your camera is bakelite, with a plastic lens).

Good reasons for having the wrong camera to hand

a) I'm between systems.
b) I'm just trying to get back to basics and improve my composition/technique.
c) I collect very bad cameras. ·
d) I'm emulating **Bert Hardy** *(q.v.)*. (In case your audience is totally ignorant or very knowledgeable it is important that you know Bert Hardy was the great *Picture Post* photographer who, irritated by people who attributed his superb results to his superb equipment, went out with a box camera and produced equally striking results.)

Good reasons for not having a camera at all

To the enthusiast there are no good reasons for not having a camera unless it has been stolen and the shops are shut.

Useful things to say to stop people asking about your camera

"What made you select that particular model?"

Carrying as it does the implication that the photographer may have made a suspect choice, this should generate a spirited defence of his or her photographic philosophy and, if time permits, their complete history of camera ownership. It is guaranteed to fill most conversational voids, especially if you are not wearing a camera.

Cameras To Be Seen With

The preferred position for a bluffer would be to have no camera, but this is socially unacceptable in photographic circles. The acceptable minimum is either to have a camera, but never be seen using it, or to buy a cheap Kodak camera case made in brown cloth, circa 1950, which you stuff with newspaper. The case is never opened under any circumstances.

If your choice is challenged, claim that you have gone back to black and white because of its greater social impact and that the capriciousness of the box camera makes greater demands. This is certain to bring nods of approval from camera buffs.

The Obsession

The major idiosyncrasy of the photographic world is its obsession with hardware, rather like people who own a vintage car.

There is always an all-pervading tendency to attribute good results to good equipment rather than its user which, if practised on a concert pianist and his or her Steinway would lead to words if not blows. This unfortunate tendency dominates the amateur's approach to the subject and can give the bluffer a major tactical advantage.

Take heart too from the fact that, unless a camera is extremely badly designed, it is capable of producing good results in most normal lighting conditions. However, if you are to be a successful bluffer it is important to have either a camera which says something about you or a very bad camera to set you apart from the crowd.

Being Tempted

One of the problems about being associated with photographers is that you may become corrupted, tempted, tainted. This corruption is seldom sexual or financial, except in the negative sense. No, the problem is that you may wish to acquire a camera or cameras beyond your needs and indeed means.

In the simple form, this affliction will lead to the acquisition of a *new* and expensive modern camera, probably a 35mm SLR, which does a number of things you do not understand, and even if you did, would never use. Numerous amateurs succumb to this.

The more extreme form involves the acquisition of an *old* and expensive camera which is a collector's piece and leads inexorably to the pursuit of all the bits for a 'system'. This extreme also involves the exchange of substantial sums of money for something which does less than the new alternative. The 'system' is similarly constrained and in many cases you can find yourself panting after a piece of gear which not only will not do what a modern automatic can, but costs more piece by piece.

There is a peripheral bonus. If you buy something new it starts to depreciate at once. If you buy the older and worthy alternative at the correct price it will in due course appreciate. There is also a certain cachet attached to its display.

It is also possible to be tempted by films. The film manufacturers would have us believe that there are discernible differences between the results obtainable from high-priced, high speed, high resolution films and their dramatically cheaper cousins. In a perfect world this is true. Alas, in an imperfect world where we all send our films to imperfect printers to be printed, it can be very difficult to tell the difference between the upmarket film and the free giveaway, once the great levelling has happened. The wise bluffer will buy on price alone and only trade up if the results are wholly unacceptable.

The World's Worst Cameras

An outsider might expect people to collect the best of the past. This does happen, and the photographic equivalent of the Stradivarius is collected avidly and at high prices. However, the *real* obsessions are about the rare and horrid. It is important to remember this before you risk comment on someone's treasured 'nasty'.

Be mildly omniscient about very bad cameras. Better still, actually own one. This virtually relieves you of the obligation to have any results. Indeed, it might be politic to buy one which is not in working order. This is even cheaper, and enables you to be permanently waiting for your little man in Soho to find the right part. Collectors will love you.

How to recognise the worst? This is a challenge. Some were unreliable; some were overpriced, some ugly, some difficult to handle, some too heavy, some too light; some were useless without batteries, some had poor lenses, some took photographs secretly in your gadget bag whenever you put them away because the shutter release was proud of the body. Others were difficult to repair when the manufacturers were still interested, and impossible thereafter. Having a unique interchangeable lens system which nobody bothered to emulate also spells trouble. It is not possible to memorise every bad camera. Instead, it should be enough to know a few examples against which to compare those you encounter in the flesh.

The first thing to remember is that no very bad cameras have been made in the Southern Hemisphere. This is because very few cameras have been manufactured south of the Equator and the scarcity affects both extremes, good and bad.

The second is that the Japanese have an unfair advantage — not that they did not make any contenders for the world's worst title, but their very commercial post-war attitudes prevented them from exporting many. Note, not 'any', because one or two horrors did in fact slip through.

Our nominee for the World's worst from Japan would be the *Plusflex*, a single lens reflex 35mm of incredibly simple specification yet with a fairly good lens aperture (which might have fooled buyers into assuming more than a shutter which doubled as a mirror) and providing only two speeds best described as slow, and dead slow.

East Germany's entry is the *Pentina*. To find out why, ask a camera repairer. They won't touch them now, and wouldn't even when contemporary spares were available. It also had a non-standard lens mount and looked chunky at a time when everyone else was trying not to.

However, **Kodak** has produced so many cameras over the years that they can be forgiven for the bluffer's pet hate — the *Kodak Instamatic 400* which had a motor-wind and slightly exposed shutter release, thereby permitting the thoughtless user to discharge a complete film without removing the camera from briefcase or handbag.

The Instamatic 126 film which that example used is common to two other nominees — precision cameras whose precision exceeded that of the film cartridges. In this category salute the *Zeiss Contaflex 126 SLR* and the *Rollei SL26*.

Nothing But The Best

These are the machines which, if you sought excellence in modern photography rather than in bluff, you might buy and use.

The oldest contemporary make is the *Gandolfi*. You can hint at an interest. The reason that you do not yet have one is, of course, that you could not make up your mind about which wood to choose and lost your place in the queue. You need to know that **Gandolfi Brothers** specialise in hand-made 10″ x 8″ cameras at their Peckham workshops. There is a two or three year waiting list. Each costs about as much as a small new car.

Coming down in size, 'medium format' is very chic. This implies negative sizes, in centimetres, of 6 x 7, 6 x 6 and 6 x 4.5. To be really chic, the *Mamiya* RZ67 is king. The reason you don't own one is not because of the price, although at c.£2000 for an acceptable kit, that might have been a factor. No, you remember the previous *RB* model. Too many faults for your liking. You are waiting for the *RZ* to settle down before you consider purchase. Note that you will *consider* purchase. Never commit to a future purchase: non-bluffers will remember. It is worth keeping in mind that the somewhat weak reservation about the RZ is also a good reason for not buying nearly any expensive new model. There is always something to dislike about the previous one.

It is vital to know that the classic medium format camera, like the current ones based on 120 or 220 film, was the twin lens reflex (TLR). It is not fashionable anymore.

Acceptable medium format names are *Hasselblad*, *Pentax* and *Bronica*. You need also know of the existence of *Plaubel Makina* and various *Rolleis*. Both these makes are less well recognised than the recent models deserve, so it is not necessary to have an opinion about them.

In 35mm format *Nikon* and *Canon* have more cachet than *Pentax,* while your position on *Olympus* must be to admire their advertisements but have no first hand opinion of the cameras. Rather like Bailey and Lichfield really.

The Best of the Rest

It is very useful to know a little about the *Leica*. It is not possible to know the lot, unless you purchase several of the vast tomes which have been written about the camera, its inventor and its makers, which will automatically disqualify you as a bluffer and turn you into an addict or enthusiast.

Here then is the essential minimum about this worthy photographic paragon. It was made by **Ernst Leitz** of Wetzlar and allegedly resulted from a private design project by their employee **Oskar Barnack.** The *Leica* system spawned a massive collection of accessories all of which are identified by five letter alphabetic coding, so a *Leica* enthusiast who is muttering about NOOKY or VIDOM, FOKOS or VIOOH, to say nothing of OOTGU and OTOOM is not practising Esperanto, and is wholly intelligible to other *Leica* addicts. Do not attempt to compete. Advanced accessory recognition will still leave you way behind unless you actually have a *Leica* around to show you belong. Instead, tell them you don't know your OOZAB from your ELPRO and leave them guessing.

Or utter the classic words from Dorothy Parker's review of *I am a Camera* variously quoted as 'No Leica' or 'Me no Leica'.

There is one other distinction. Just as '*Leica* screw' is not an informal invitation, so '*Leica* Bayonet' is not a

14

warlike one. The early *Leicas* had screw-mounted interchangeable lenses. For purists these are the only real *Leicas* and the later ones with bayonet mounts are distinctly less worthy. Much later ones in which the rangefinder method of focus control had given way to the single lens reflex method, are of course beyond the pale.

Hasselblad, is the Swedish camera industry's only claim to fame. *Hasselblad* users are likely to be professional photographers, very rich amateurs, or astronauts whose cameras have been lent to them by mission control.

The Swiss ought to have a camera which represents their watch-making history and their famous clinical attitudes. The *Alpa,* by **Pignons S.A.** is the only significant recent Swiss camera — an excellent SLR. Alas, the most collectable Swiss camera, made by the watchmakers Le Coultre, was not a commercial success and was British designed. Anyone using one is likely to be a British collector rather than a refugee from the land of yodelling and mountain horns.

There are relatively few American cameras and even less great ones, but the use of any of them tells you a lot about the owner. If you consider first the cheap and cheerful category with things like basic *Kodaks,* *Keystone* and perhaps the simpler *Bell and Howells* you can assume that the user is concerned only with function and, to his or her credit, is not a camera snob.

Those using early *Ansco* or *Argus,* (which looks like a brick) are of course collectors, while the *Polaroid* user may be rank amateur or hardy professional. If you ever come across something which the owner's proud bearing implies is a modern camera, but looks like a small piano-accordion or a First World War tank, that is a

Polaroid. Polaroid cameras enable you to take bad photographs fairly quickly — that is to say there has to be a longer interval between pictures than you would expect with a motorwind but you can see how horrid the results are soon enough to tempt you to try for a better picture. This sells a lot of film, which is a good thing for **Polaroid Land Corporation,** considering their film prices by comparison with non-instant materials.

Instant pictures also appeal to those who wish to take photographs of their loved ones, or someone else's, in states of extreme undress and indeed extreme bad taste without embarrassing the staff of commercial photo processors. This is a euphemism for not embarrassing the photographers — the processors are well beyond embarrassment and close to terminal levity. With luck, instant pictures may also tempt those with some artistic sense into thinking again; not, as the film manufacturers might hope, into taking more shots until you get it right but about giving the whole thing up altogether. Only with instant pictures does the awesome gap between reality and real life loom so quickly and graphically.

On this front, *Polaroids* have enabled the professional photographers to fight back at Art Directors. Most medium format professional cameras have *Polaroid backs* which enable test shots to be made before the actual pictures are taken. The client disappointed with the final results is now reminded firmly that their Art Director 'agreed the Polaroids'.

Another good name is **Folmer and Schwing**. They sound like a pair of psychiatrists who have written a noted book. In fact they were the proprietors of the firm which made the *Speed Graphic,* the definitive big press camera. Anyone using a *Speed Graphic* is not a press photographer or is trying to look like one, so is presumably an actor.

The use of a Russian camera tells you very little about its carrier except that he or she is unlikely to be a Russian spy. They are likely to be impoverished amateurs or possibly people seeking an innocuous but effective blunt instrument to use as defence in a street fight. The *Fed*, *Kiev*, *Zenit* and *Zorki* fall into this category. Most are copies of something the West did better.

In the hardly-visible-at-all group comes the superb *Minox*, a sub-miniature which was once to be seen in all the best spy films and as a result is most unlikely to be seen with a real spy. The only thing you can deduce from the use of a 'real' *Riga Minox* is that the owner is a collector. Intelligence agencies have for some years preferred good 35mm miniatures — formerly good rangefinder models, and nowadays workmanlike 35mm SLRs. Both are good for document copying.

You may be certain that anyone using a British precision camera these days must be a reactionary or a collector. The British camera industry went into terminal decline in the postwar years and almost all those firms producing cameras since 1945 have given up. Other dead names include *Agilux*, *Corfield*, *Dufay*, *MPP*, *Reid and Sigrist*, *Purma* and *Wray*. All of them spell collector. *Purma* also spells eccentric. (It had a gravity assisted shutter which clunked rather than clicked every trip.) Do not forget *Ilford*, the old faithful of British cameras — most of them sound and pedestrian with just a few remarkably nice ones, like the *Advocate* and *Witness*.

Finally, two unexpected names. *Nimslo* is the first. You could claim that the Nimslo owner is not a photographer in the eyes of other photographers or even bluffers, although history may prove us wrong. *Kodak* is the second. There were a few excellent precision *Kodaks* which you might still find attached to a discriminating owner. The *Retina* and perhaps *Retina Reflex* qualify.

The *Retinette* does not.

You may care to point out that the *Kodaks* mentioned above were actually made in Germany, therefore the discerning American national would until recently have been found with a German camera. He is now likely to be wearing a Japanese one.

Which Camera Did What First

This is an area where the bluffer can establish massive moral superiority, not just by knowing who was first but by knowing which popular candidate was *not*. It can also be great fun because the popular choices are seldom right. Good public relations and/or advertising have conveyed fallacious impressions, probably because most people in the public relations and advertising world are bluffing too. Wilful ignorance seems to be the philosophy wherever facts conflict with client needs.

Motordrive is a good example. Agfa spent large sums of money announcing the world's first compact motorwind camera and had to be reminded by the Advertising Standards Authority that Robot did it first, in 1934. Robot enthusiasts, who tend to be very keen on examples with swastikas and other Germanic military insignia all over them, do not care to be reminded that the *Debrie Sept* was earlier (in 1922), but not so compact.

Polaroid instant cameras are also regarded as the first examples of instant photography. Alas, at least one and possibly two processes preceded them. **Jules Bourdain**'s is the better process to quote. To console *Polaroid* aficionados you may inform them that Polaroid did produce the first electronic shutter, as this fact may have passed them by. It was the American **Dr. Edwin Land** who invented both. Prophets are without honour in their own time when that time honours profits more.

The bluffer should also note for quotation the fact that the recent litigation by *Polaroid* which removed Kodak's instant picture range from the market was *Kodak*'s second disappointment in this field. The first was their frustration at being the inventors of relatively instant pictures for use during the Second World War, but debarred from producing a commercial system because the Government applied its '30 year rule'. In consequence Polaroid Land were able to capture the post-war market.

Asahi Pentax is widely regarded as the first name in instant return mirrors. You can irritate all *Pentax* owners by pointing out that historians attribute this honour to the 1947 *Gamma Duflex*, although it was hardly a commercial success. *Pentax* owners are not overjoyed either by the fact that the so-called *Pentax* screw mount was actually introduced by *Praktica*. In fact most of the things which proud *Pentax* owners claim as Asahi firsts turn out to be Asahi seconds, but done better or more widely than the innovators. Pentax were third with the pentaprism viewfinder (the thing which gives a right way up, right way round image in the viewfinder). *Contax* and *Alpa* were 1st and 2nd. Pentax owners are sitting ducks, because they are even prepared to believe that Asahi introduced the first TTL (through the lens) metering when it is a matter of record that the *Topcon RE Super* did it a year earlier. You can also remind *Pentax* or *Leica* owners that *Leica* (with its Astroflex reflex box attachment between lens and body in 1933) has a tenuous claim to the first 35mm SLR although the Russian *Sport* may have been the first built-in example, closely followed by the *Kine-Exacta* in 1936. The merits of this particular claim are that it annoys the Asahi crowd by identifying yet another area where they were not first and reminds the *Leica* people that they were almost first with the SLR principle which later destroyed their market when it was done properly by others.

Further salt in the *Leica* wound can be poured by mentioning the first use of 35mm film in a still camera. *Leica* fans will usually claim this was theirs, pioneered by Oskar Barnack. You need only point to the 1912 *Homeos* to refute this and can turn the knife in the wound by adding the 1922 *Debrie Sept*. *Leica* didn't get rolling with a production model until 1925. Having established a clear lead, you can then permit the *Leica* team their one point for the first interchangable lens in 35mm cameras.

Other useful firsts include:

- *Hasselblad* - first on the moon and left there, to save weight on the return journey, not as ungracious owners might suggest because the extras to keep it up to date are so costly.

- *Focaflex* - the French contender for worlds most irritating SLR which with true Gallic independence used a simple mirror prism rather than a pentaprism so that the image is reversed as on a TLR, although the casual buyer might assume the presence of a normal system - the UK price certainly implied this.

- *Nimslo* - for trying to make stereo sandwich prints popular. Traditionally most pioneers fail financially. So did they.

The Great Ar Mystery

There is a mysterious practice, nearly a century old, which may actually enhance your position just by knowing the question without the answer. Fortunately no contemporary answer is needed as the Japanese have drifted away from it altogether.

We refer to the 'ar' suffix which is appended to the names of so many great lenses without reason.

Numerous manufacturers have followed the pattern. Examples included Apotar, Biloxar, Cassar, Dignar, Elmar, Finetar, Graftar, Hexar, Industar, Kalmar, Lypar, Mirar, Noritar, Optar, Paxanar, Radionar, Summar, Tessar, Uitar, Westar, Xenar and Secanar.

The bluffer can learn something about a camera from the name of the lens. If the initial letter of the name is the same as the initial letter of the camera it is almost certain that both lens and camera are pretty mediocre.

Very good cameras have lenses which have an identity of their own and it is statistically unlikely that there is going to be a coincidence of intitials. *Pentax* has Takumar, *Olympus* has Zuiko, *Leica* has Elmar, *Voigtländer* has Lanthar.

The most honest name for an undistinguished lens must be the Cute Anastigmat, which at least left the user in no doubt as to its limitations.

If someone knowledgeable, or ungracious, calls your bluff and gives you a reason why all were 'ar's-ended, you should ask your informant why all the other great lenses end in 'on' and 'or'.

The Question Of Colour

This has nothing to do with colour film or the colour of people. It is about cameras. The first issue concerns the vexed question of bodies. White is out, except on a few vintage models. Real gold is definitely out unless one was given a gold one by the manufacturers for being such a good photographer. So are animal skins (snake, mink or otherwise). But most important, all colours which look right for boats lost ot sea (orange, red, yellow, etc.) are wrong for real cameras. This is because cameras finished in vivid colours may reflect on to the subject and thus produce unnatural hues in the photographs.

The key choice is therefore between chrome and black. Most standard finishes are black *and* chrome but the status element increases as the total volume of chrome reduces, and the black increases. An all black camera, made thus by the manufacturers, is the hallmark of the very serious amateur and some professionals.

Slightly upmarket of this is the mixed chrome/black example with the chrome bits hand-painted matt black. This spells dedicated amateur or the professional who is important enough not to care and does not have to answer to a newspaper for the equipment. The finishing touch in this scale is the odd spot of white paint on all the dials at the most commonly used settings. Definitely the ultimate professional image or superb fakery.

The second issue involves grey imports. These are cameras, or other expensive hardware, which have been imported from a territory where:

a) the new retail price is substantially lower than that at home, or

b) the wholesale price is lower and bulk supplies can be shifted readily across national boundaries.

Usually the movement is perfectly legal but the UK importers disapprove and attempt to discourage the erosion of their profits by disqualifying these units for guarantee purposes. So beware.

How To Wear Your Camera

There is a very unfortunate tendency among people who should know better to hang a camera with a long (telephoto or zoom) lens at waist level. A little thought would suggest to them that this is not only vulgar but sexist. The fact that it is virtually impossible for the thing to stay level, so that it droops in an unprepossessing way, is even more depressingly symbolic.

The alternative is to use something called a warthog. This is rather like a sporran which has lost all its fur and, when in use, looks as if you are carrying a spare haggis about your person. It can also look like a codpiece, if the designer was so inclined or the beholder has a nasty mind. On balance, the naked equipment looks better.

There are several other socially acceptable ways to wear a camera. For the gentle reader we recommend something small, on a wrist strap, or the conventional SLR on the neck strap adjusted so the machine is at chest level. If you have a big one there are chunky things called gadget bags which hang from the shoulder at hip level and look fairly 'professional'.

In actual fact the true pro does not sport a camera at all. If it is 35mm it may be left in the glove compartment of the car until required, ignoring the old wives/journalists warnings about the sustained heat being bad for the film. (The warning is valid, but professionals use film fast enough for the dose to be limited, by comparison with the amateur's which lingers for weeks unused.) Pros relegate larger formats to a large aluminium case, strong enough to stand on, and designed to cause the maximum pain to a West Ham striker who has just beaten the goalie, missed a sitter, and crashed into it on the touchline to gain sympathy from the crowd. Other than this, the pro will only carry a compact if:

a) he senses the possibility of a 'grab shot' when otherwise off duty, or
b) he is attending an event thrown by the makers of
   the compact who pay him large sums to be seen
   waving it about.

Carrying two cameras may seem only a step away from
the suspect amateurs who spend 'glamour weekends'
with three or more models slung round their paunches,
but it is respectable to have a second camera or second
body for your 'system' for one or more of the following
reasons:

a) so you have colour and monochrome available
b) for different film speeds
c) for instant access to standard and telephoto (or
   wide-angle and telephoto)
d) so that at least one foolproof camera can be brought
   into action quickly.

If you've got it, flaunt it, unless you are in a country
where the mobile thieves snatch anything of value and
depart at high speed on scooters. We can imagine few
things more ignominious than being towed by the neck
on one's Pentax Wide Strap while the thief attempts to
detach it from the camera, or you from the strap.

GETTING IT RIGHT

What's Wrong and Why

As with aviation and computers, most faults in photography arise from human error. In the case of cameras the fault is usually 'pilot error' rather than that of a distant third party.

The bluffer can gain a distinguished and not wholly deserved reputation as an omniscient diagnostician with many cameras simply by reading the instructions, because most owners are to lazy to do so. They will even put you ahead of the *Reader's Digest Repair Manual*, although this is not difficult as the contents are overly concerned with cleaning and mending holes in the camera bellows. If however the instructions are not available, or you are too lazy to read them, the following examples may by helpful.

- Many 35mm cameras 'won't rewind', when the film has finished. You can win points by suggesting that the rewind button has not been depressed. If it has been, push it harder.
- Others 'won't wind on' which can mean several things. It could be that the user has failed to set the exposure counter correctly or even to read it, and the film is finished. Check by feeling whether there is any slack at the rewind knob or crank. If not, this diagnosis is confirmed. The alternative is that the previous exposure did not take place, i.e. the shutter release was not fully depressed so the camera is preventing the user winding on and thus wasting an unused section of film.
- Another thing the generalist manuals do not tell you is that 'nothing works' is a deliberate symptom when a planned safety feature has come into play. For ex-

ample, manufacturers have been known to arrange this feature in the following circumstances:

a) No film or film finished
b) No batteries, or faded ones
c) Lens retracted in carrying position (*Leica, Purma,* etc.)
d) Lens cap still on (rare device but useful)
e) Delayed action set
f) Film chamber not fully closed
g) Insufficient light for automatic exposure to work
h) Shutter lock set
i) Flash not yet fully recharged.

The choice dictates trial and error but you can look exceptionally experienced while fiddling.

● 'The shutter is jammed' can be due to the previous causes but it can also cover:

a) with old cameras, failure to wind the shutter (which was not coupled to the film wind in most pre-war and some post-war types)
b) also in old cameras, trying to set the shutter speed after the shutter has been wound. Bluffers gain kudos by, very gently, moving the speed dial back to the original setting if this is possible, or by firing the shutter with the lens cap on and then resetting the shutter correctly. Howls of derision may emerge from non-bluffers at this point because they don't know that you have depressed the rewind button to avoid wasting film while you wound on the shutter.

For all other mysterious malfunctions which do not actually involve bits dropping off the camera (or in modern ones, wisps of smoke) the correct procedure is to go through the normal SAFEWay routine, i.e.

Set shutter speed
Adjust aperture of lens
Focus on subject
Expose film
Wind on — and away you go again.

Gentle repetition will usually solve the problem. Whatever the cause, never be tempted to dismantle or oil the machine. Modern cameras do not need oiling and they reassemble far less readily than they dismantle.

Finally, if the camera is your own or the owner is out of sight, there are two alternative sovereign remedies. One is to fetch the beast a sharp slap, manually, if it is mechanical rather than electric or electronic. The other, for battery powered examples, is to remove, clean and replace the batteries IN THE CORRECT DIRECTION. You are now more than halfway to being an expert. Recommending professional repair takes care of the rest.

Do's and Don'ts

Take comfort from the fact that you do not have to be a photographer at all to obtain moral ascendancy over most amateurs and quite a few professionals.

It is perfectly permissible to be able to take photographs, but perhaps less acceptable to let third parties see the results. However, it is very important to know why other people, professional or otherwise, take bad photographs and even good ones.

Always point out that results depend on the photographer and not on the cameras so that having a very expensive product hung round your neck, or indeed any other part of your anatomy, can be counter-productive. The ownership of a top-of-range camera which produces bottom of range results tells the world quite a lot about your competence.

When defending your position as:

a) a non camera owner, or
b) the owner of a non-prestige camera, or
c) a prestige camera of yesteryear which is wholly
   manual

remind the critic that advanced cameras, unless totally automatic, merely offer extra ways of getting things wrong.

You could also mention that avoiding error is an important part of good photography. This may not win you friends but will retain your moral superiority. Moral superiority is rather important because criticism of photographs, unlike criticism of works of art, is likely to take place in the presence of the perpetrator. Even when looking at the work of a professional in a gallery or other exhibition, there is a strong possibility that he or she may be among those present. So take heed of what you can, and indeed should, criticise about other people's efforts. In the process you may, by osmosis, learn how to take photographs which are quite presentable.

Basic Errors

The things which ruin amateur snaps are not necessarily wrong when done by professionals. Paradoxically, the fact that the professionals do them and get away with it demonstrates their professionalism or, according to your point of view, their sheer brass nerve. Rather like the cave man who invented cooked meat — an accident turned to advantage. Some professional photographs look like that and it is perfectly acceptable to say so if the photographer isn't around. However, if he or she is in the vicinity you may have to do better than smart remarks about accidents in the Stone Age. The correct technique is to know the accident which produced the result on view. Accidents know no boundaries of professionalism. The symptoms are almost invariably the same. Do not discuss the symptoms. The only safe comment is a factual statement of the error which produced the allegedly artistic result you are being shown — such as:

a) If the whole picture is uniformly blurred you can almost invariably deduce 'camera shake'. It is permissible to mention this to friends and relations. You can also mention that it can be cured by using faster shutter speed and/or holding the camera more steadily. It is not appropriate to make this comment to professionals. They have tripod spikes.

b) If the blurring is partial, with the subject blurred and the foreground or background sharp, the diagnosis is 'incorrect focus' and anyone willing to receive advice may be told to switch to a camera with rangefinder or reflex focussing. Or to guess better.

c) If the print or slide is much too dark, you may mutter 'under-exposed'. Then recommend using an exposure meter or even the chart which usually comes with each film.

d) A washed out result — much too light, indicates 'over-exposure' but the solution is the same.

All the above have at some time or another been used, perhaps deliberately by photographers in search of special effects — or excuses.

e) The same applies to the 'ghost' effect produced by double exposure, when two pictures are taken on one piece of film. This cannot happen by accident with modern cameras or earlier precision models, so anyone claiming to have done it deliberately with a recent camera is likely to be telling the truth and should not be lightly contradicted.

f) The total absence of a picture may mean several things. You could explain that it is due to taking pictures with the lens cap on (not possible if they are using a single lens reflex) or, with an older camera, that they have wound the film on twice without firing the shutter, so that the result is a clear negative or a totally black slide. Shutter failure can do this too. If the whole film is like this, they have failed to load the film properly. The reverse symptom, a totally black negative or clear slide, results from the failure to wind the (35mm) film back into the cassette after the last exposure.

You will not catch professionals displaying this sort of error, even to friends.

g) Random fogging, or ruination can be simply the result of travelling by air. Remind others that any security system for baggage based on low dose Xrays may ruin a film both before or after exposure.

More fundamental errors are still possible. There is a marvellous cartoon which shows a supercilious camera dealer saying to a puzzled customer 'Of course Sir cannot find out where to put the film in . . . Sir is holding an electric razor.'

Composition

Composition is the area which sorts out the good amateurs and the professionals from the rest. As with music there are some basic rules of composition which the amateurs ignore at their peril and the really good photographers flout with success.

The golden rule for criticism in the area of composition is twofold. If it looks wrong it almost certainly *is* wrong and you can find a classic error to reinforce your criticism. However, if the picture has such a 'classic' error but it looks right, the photographer is competent, perhaps even gifted. Think before you speak.

A few examples should make this clearer. Posed amateur snaps generally look awful, yet several distinguished photographers have either managed to pose the subjects so that they don't look posed or have used the formality of the pose to add dignity and impact. Amateur 'glamour' doesn't need any clues to identify it. Its total lack of artistic or erotic impact is sufficient guide.

People gazing into the lens (not necessarily posed) generally look wrong. Only the competent photographer can get away with this. Similarly a subject dead centre in the photograph is wrong in theory according to camera clubs and arty writers but is actually exactly what the professional photographer wants and the amateur or bluffer can learn from this. Subjects dead centre come from good photographers.

Very simple things like getting the horizon correct are also important and the bluffer can use this as a standard weapon.

Finally, never criticise anyone else's work directly. Merely hint at the good practice which appears to be lacking in the print in question. For instance, if the lighting lacks something, state with truth that "The right lighting is *so* important for good results." It may occasionally be taken as a compliment but at least this tactic avoids direct conflict. Bluffers are allowed to be cowards, by the way.

Lulling Suspicions

Most people are relatively ignorant about photography and, though at first startled by the appearance of a person with a camera close at hand, will quickly resume their former activities, particularly while drinking. There are some similarities with wild life photography here. The calming effect is heightened if the intruder is neutrally dressed and the camera is dark, battered and without flash equipment. It is not generally realised that with modern films (400/1000 ASA) and a decent lens (f/2 or better) it is perfectly feasible to take good pictures, hand-held, by candlelight, provided the subject is close to the light source. Better still, in similar circumstances the victims assume there is no danger because your flash has not gone off and you may become a subject for mild badinage. When you show them the candid pictures which result this may become worsinage.

In daylight the same simple attitudes also help. Because snapshot family photographers always point their cameras directly at the victim with the grim determination of a firing squad and condition the subject to face the lens in the same manner (and attitude of mind) most previous victims will not be alarmed if you point the camera ten degrees to the left or right, particularly if they are not looking at you. This has two advantages:

1. The results are more natural
2. The composition is better because when the subject is looking sideways in a picture the viewer's mind is happier if the subject seems to be looking across the frame, rather than out of it.

Choice of camera can also help. So many modern cameras have to be held to the eye to focus and shoot that anything with a waist level viewfinder is assumed to be out of action. This applies to all TLRs, a few SLRs and some old box and folding cameras with external reflex finders.

Doing it Better

Successful performance as a bluffer inevitably leads to being asked for advice by an admiring relative. These notes are for your guidance when the nephew or niece needs guidance.

It may be helpful to ascend to a high philosophical plane. Point out that photography is all about recording the visible effects of light and shade, colour and shades of grey, events and non-events, action and still life.

The typical relative will at this point drag you back to basics and ask for advice on cameras. Your safest posture is qualified disapproval, no matter what they have in their hands. You can then help them to make the best of a bad job.

For example, the likelihood is that he/she has been given or has bought a compact. Your view must be that the sole merit of a compact is that it is compact. Compact 35mm cameras have only two other minor advantages. First, that they take 35mm cassettes, which give the most varied choice of film type possible. Second, that their short focal length lenses eliminate the need for precise focussing.

Alas, they have compensating disadvantages. The short focal length actually means that you have a permanent wide angle lens fitted. This is not an extra bonus, it is a disaster. Casual study of the photographic media will reveal that when photographers of all grades, shapes and sizes buy extra lenses, zoom or telephoto, what they want is a telephoto facility. Relatively few seek wider angles. Observe the modern press photographer too; those pendulous things on the front of their cameras are without exception there to get in close, not to widen the field of view. All the great photographers of the past, when coaxed for advice to amateurs insisted that getting closer, on foot or with telephoto lens, is crucial.

Your protegé may protest that this makes it impossible to photograph groups properly. Point out that only wedding photographers have to photograph groups. Nobody else should.

Recommend architecture instead. At least with a building you can wait until the time of day when the sun comes round to an ideal positition and the textures or the shadows make an acceptable pattern. The sun very seldom does this with groups of aunties. By all means suggest people in photographs of buildings, they help to give an impression of scale, but not close enough to the camera to be dominant.

Remind the amateur that verticals tend to converge, and that unless he or she is actually seeking to demonstrate that effect, there are several easy cures — without resorting to the special lenses and rising fronts of technical cameras, as follows:-

a) move back a bit
b) use a wide-angle lens
c) climb up something
d) turn the camera at right angles so the picture area is upright rather than horizontally biased, i.e. 'portrait' rather than landscape format.

Failing a suitable collection of bricks and mortar, suggest a candle-lit experiment, if only because it is likely to be an indoor portrait and everyone should try portraits, however informally, at some stage. It also teaches amateurs something about themselves. Quote **Baron**, the portrait photographer, who said 'To be a successful portraitist either your photography must be good or you must have sufficient personality to direct the sitter. You can get along with either but you must have one or the other.' This is, indirectly, another good reason for avoiding groups.

Portraits also provide a chance to turn the camera on end and use the frame vertically. A great many pictures are ruined because the photographer fails to appreciate this simple possibility. It can help to get closer, too.

Remember to stress the fact that photographs have impact because of light and colour, seldom because of the subject alone. Set your pupil a small task — to go away and fill a whole reel, roll, cassette or cartridge of film solely with pictures that have visual impact, i.e.

- a splash of colour in an otherwise drab picture
- a splodge of black in a colourful one
- a sharply focussed subject contrasting with an out-of-focus background or foreground (easy to achieve by using a wide aperture)
- texture or patterns
- arrested motion
- a visual joke or anomaly.

This has two advantages. It will save a lot of film, and you may not be bothered for days, if not weeks, thereafter.

Film

In order to bluff better, and for the benefit of nieces and nephews, you must recognise that bluff can conflict with practicality. The arch bluffer would undoubtedly carry bulk stock of low speed, fine grain monochrome film. This screams to the informed viewer that the user does his own processing and has a precision camera capable of recording high-quality images on the high quality film. The practical amateur, on the other hand, is going to plump for a medium or fairly high speed colour film which a professional laboratory can process at modest cost. The 100-400 ASA range covers most needs.

State that there isn't a great deal to choose between film makes unless you are going for very expensive specialist types. The unashamed amateur can legitimately buy almost any make of colour film which is going cheap, if 'in date', confident that the processing house's competence, or lack thereof, makes more difference than the film.

Advise against buying very short lengths (this applies to 110, 126 and 35mm but not to 120) because the cost per exposure is disproportionately high and the cost of processing makes matters worse. Only at the 20/24 exposure mark does the cost of film and processing get down to an economic level. Recommend also that they do not leap from one film speed to another without good reason, not only because it is so easy to leave the exposure control set to the wrong speed (impossible with DX coding, which reads the speed off the film itself, but this is still rare) but also because sticking to the same speed, make and type makes for more consistent results.

Finally, advocate prints rather than slides, both because you detest the slide show trap, and because the hardware with which you project the stuff is never as good as the hardware you took it with and therefore doesn't do it justice. This is bunk of course if the camera is simple, but it is a useful throwaway line.

And don't forget to mention that Kodachrome, the most important colour film of the century, was invented by two musicians, Godowsky and Mannes. Why they were fiddling with photo-chemistry no one knows, but they obviously followed in the great tradition of Victorian amateurs.

The Image

All of us have suffered at the hands of the amateur photographer with snaps or slides to show. There are ways to avoid these persons, but they offer an exemplary lesson. Determine that you are not going to be like them. Nobody should have to leaf through dozens of bad colour prints or sit yawning through a slide show.

Defending Yourself

First, how to avoid being shown them. For prints, there are two levels of defence. Not having your reading glasses will stop anyone who doesn't know you don't need them. If this excuse won't wash, you have to train them for the future by riffling quickly through the pack with absolutely no sign of interest and commenting benevolently on the most common fault you can identify, before you change the subject. Most people won't show you the next batch.

Slides are a different matter. If the proud owner proffers them by hand, displayed against the nearest light source, either of the above techniques may be relevant. At least there is unlikely to be more than one box at a time. Alas, the high-tech fiend with an automatic slide projector is more determined and will have row upon row of magazines full of the unedited results of a summer's snapping and, with worse luck, the winter's as well.

Short of sabotaging the projector (it is not well known that you can 'blow' most projector bulbs by shaking the projector firmly, when switched on) the excuses have to be pretty good.

An obscure eye condition which reacts badly to viewing bright screens in darkened rooms is first class. You can do your own research, but the Posner-Schlossman syndrome is worth quoting if you can't find one you like. It has the advantage that its symptoms occur unpredictably and it is chronic. The second excuse might be to feign the symptoms of narcolepsy and/or perfect a revolting snore.

As a final defence against the interminable amateur show, make sure that when the owner hands you a prized but horrid transparency or print, you grasp it so that either thumb or forefinger is planted firmly on the emulsion. This will curtail the session quicker than any known method.

Fighting Back

Enough of defence. Now for attack. To obtain more professional results, you must adopt the tricks of the trade. Professionals, unless they are wedding photographers, have one great advantage over the amateur which is seldom recognised or indeed mentioned. They hide or destroy the majority of their work. If you are prepared to do the same, the quality of your 'published' results can take a great leap forward.

Consider the results you will achieve if you do not:
a) No result — 'it didn't come out'
b) Bad composition and technique
c) Bad composition, good technique
d) Good composition, bad technique
e) Good composition, good technique

It should go without saying that you don't show people things in the first category. It is an easy step to exclude the (b) examples. The difficulty the amateur faces is that much of the normal output then falls under (c) and (d). We suggest, very strongly, that your aim should be to steel yourself to scrap or at least suppress the work in these categories, even though it leaves very little available for display under (e). Heart-rending though this may be, it brings enormous benefits.

- It must force you try harder, sooner, to get things right.
- It reduces the risk that you will lose friends by being a photobore.
- It dramatically improves your reputation as a photographer.

Display

As for the display of prints, the expert will put the minority of good ones in an album. Modern albums with self-adhesive pages and a transparent covering sheet for each page give you control over the way people see the results. But the crucial professional trick is to crop the finished prints to a size and shape which enhances the composition. For this you really need one essential extra piece of hardware — a small guillotine.

Professional Conduct

Photography is not an area where all the professionals are professional about their conduct (with the results, not the subjects).

The ethical guidelines may be paraphrased as follows, although some manage to achieve higher standards than these basic ones:

1. Make sure what you are doing is legal.
2. If not, don't get found out.
3. If caught, make sure that the medium in which you are published will defend you and can afford to, come what may.
4. Get 'model release' forms signed, giving you the subject's permission to do almost anything with the results. See her birth certificate.
5. In extremis be prepared to affirm that "Candid photography is an essential constituent of a free press in a free society". This one cannot be used world-wide.
6. Only pinch your colleagues' work when they are away in a war zone.
7. Always insist that the negatives belong to the photographer, despite the fact that the client has paid for them.

SPECIALIST SUBJECTS

Aerial

Our forefathers (and in some cases foremothers) were obsessed with the idea of photography from a great height. They achieved this in the 19th century with the aid of tall buildings, cliffs, mountains and, as science marched on, balloons, kites and long pieces of rope suspended between two high places.

In this century better balloons, gliders, model aircraft, autogyros and helicopters have all been pressed into service. Today it's done from space.

Equally, it is remarkable what a tall crane and a wide-angle lens can do. Always scan the print for a telltale shadow.

Real aerial photography can nowadays be identified by a regression in the technical quality of the print, designed to remind us that the photographer was hanging upside down from the harness in someone else's Pitt Special biplane at the time, so that we should be honoured that he has produced anything at all.

Advertising Photography

As with television advertising, the quality of the product in still photography for advertising use is dramatically better than that on editorial pages because there is more money and time to apply to it, pro rata.

Alas, the geniuses who produce these results seldom get credit. They are the equivalent of the 'session man' in the music recording world who are uncredited, unseen and in all senses unsung.

The bluffer is entitled to say that things ain't what

they used to be. In the sixties the finest photographers were all in advertising or on the fringes. Most have now moved on. This is because the Art Director and Stylist have taken over (hi-jacked) the business. The so-called photographer's sole function nowadays is to provide a large and very expensive space in the West End, a massive flash lighting unit and a 10″ x 8″ camera with a *Polaroid back*. The final transparency has to be practically a facsimile of the Art Director's rough (his major concern is where to put his text). The Stylist sets the whole shot up. The models are chosen by the Advertising Agency and the ultimate snobbery is that the assistant (usually hired for the day) loads the camera and fires the shutter.

The advertising photographer today could be described as little more than a technical advisor. Test shots done free by the professionals when testing new lighting techniques and films are the only area where the pro can express himself and have complete control.

Estate Agents' Photography

This is a specialised branch of the art, readily identified by these key characterisitics:

a) The gasometer behind the house was in thick low cloud at the time.

b) The best car in the district was parked in front of the house moments before the photograph was taken (and was removed moments later because the estate agent who owns it knows it isn't safe to leave lavish motors around there unattended).

c) Not one house in the whole of London or the South East seems to have a single or double yellow line outside it.

d) The agent owns a telephoto lens, so that decent shots can be obtained from long distance of houses too close to the railway/dual carriageway/bus/school/local lunatic asylum.

Even bluffers do not explore this photographic cul-de-sac.

Fashion Photography

This is the one area that gives a photographer a chance of becoming a household name. **Richard Avedon**, **David Bailey**, **Cecil Beaton**, **Norman Parkinson** and **John French** are all names to quote in this context. But to get right to the top you must be part of the scene. Those who are in or near *Vogue*, Wedgies, and the gossip columns of the *Express* and *Mail* are part of this scene. A direct line to television is also a good indicator of burgeoning success.

There is also excellent unsung work being done by the anonymous producers of models' walker-cards or composites. This only earns *them* fame, but may be the photographer's stepping stone to fortune.

Micro, Macro Photography

Photomacrography, now called macrophotography (by specialist journalists who are attempting to achieve in the photographic press the same standards which *Sun* saboteurs are instilling at *The Times*) uses a normal lens on a very long extension. Useful for insects not visible to the naked eye.

Photomicrography is not a spelling error. It is that

which is miscalled microphotography these days and represents a chance for the bluffer to demonstrate an understanding of the difference between this and 'macro'. It involves using camera and microscope in conjunction. The results are usually unrecognisable. Something which looks in a print like a hairy telephone cord is almost certainly to do with communications — the living form of a communicable disease in all probability.

Nude Photography

Many young males take up photography for two reasons only:

1. They are genuinely interested in the subject
2. It is another route to engaging the attention of the prettier members of the opposite sex.

The latter are the most numerous. For some inexplicable reason pretty girls are attracted to photographers like moths to a flame. This is not male chauvinist fantasy, it is actually true. The better the photographer becomes at making a pretty girl prettier, the more popular he becomes.

Once he is proficient, the next step (and the point of the whole exercise) is to get a female to disrobe, without cost. At this point the bluffer has a problem. The essence of the bluff is to avoid using film, but the female of the species is going to be adamant about seeing results, so you have only three choices:

a) get professional very quickly
b) propose marriage
c) lie about the failure of the hardware or process.

Paparazzi

It is worth bearing in mind, if this area appeals to you, that paparazzi seldom earn vast sums of money, even if they are good. The most famous product, the nude of Jackie Onassis, cost a disproportionate slice of the take in man hours, boat hire, middleman's fees and non-payment of reproduction fees.

It is infinitely more entertaining to become adept at spotting which of their shots are careful set-ups contrived and manipulated by the publicity conscious and the not-so-famous.

War Photography

Another area best avoided. Photographers such as **Don McCullin** are not only brave but very talented. Do not under any circumstances mix with them. It is useful to know that the camera has changed man's attitude towards war in general. The Americans made the great mistake of losing control of photographic images in Vietnam and lost. The British demanded complete control in the Falklands and won.

This branch of photography wins prizes. It is also highly dangerous. Being assaulted by the heavy minders of celebrities is a trifle compared to the (terminal) assaults inflicted on the modern war cameraman. In the old days, **Brady**, **Forrest**, **Capa** and the like could assume that their equipment marked them as non-combatants. Nowadays there is a strong possibility that photographic equipment proclaims you as a media lackey of the Western Capitalists. 'Fair game' is the short version.

PROCESS PIONEERS

Learning about the early days of photography can leave you with a faint sense that somebody is having you on. Not so. You can relay this information with a straight face and a clear conscience.

The first 'camera' was the 'camera obscura' which it is said that **Ibn Al-Haitham** was using in 1038. This consisted of a light-tight room with a very small hole in one wall, presumably discovered by accident or an early peeping Tom, who observed that an image of the scene outside formed on the opposite wall. Lenses later improved the result but nobody successfully recorded the image, except by tracing it, until the early 19th century.

There is a good reason for this. Until someone thought to incorporate a mirror into the setup it had to be viewed upside down and there must be a limit to the enthusiasm one can generate for any view while bent double with one's head at stomach level.

The next practical hurdle remains even now. After waiting many hundreds of years to record the results produced by 'the camera' most pioneers could only find materials which darkened on exposure to light rather than bleached out, thereby ensuring that photography was trapped into using negative images and cumbersome processes for all time.

The things the early experimenters did in their darkrooms, or in some cases, in public, defy logical analysis. There is also an illogical mixture of speed and sloth about developments which deferred the introduction of some very basic improvements for many decades.

The way to fix the pioneers in your mind is to recall the peculiarly odious materials they used. There is no record of the processes which failed but some of the passing successes make one wonder what the instant failures were like.

Thomas Wedgwood was using a camera of sorts in 1802, but could not 'fix' his pictures. He and **Humphry Davy** used a solution of silver nitrate applied to paper or white leather, which darkened on exposure to light (a fact recorded first by **Angelo Sola** in 1614). These experiments must have been hard on the local sources of leather because the image simply vanished on fuller exposure to light.

It is to the Frenchman, **Joseph Nicéphore Niepce** that the credit is given for taking the first photograph, in 1826. This was of a view from his window and took eight hours to expose. The image of the window, ironically, is more memorable than the subject it framed. As not even the French can agree upon how to pronounce his surname, and they managed to erect a monument to him with the wrong date on it, you can be excused from a clear understanding of Niepce's process, which involved pewter plates soaked in oil of lavender, and bitumen of Judea.

He later worked closely with **Daguerre**, a scene painter for the theatre, who used a silver-plated copper sheet previously exposed to iodine vapour, exposing this to the light, developing the image by using mercury vapour and 'fixing' the (positive) image permanently thereafter. These materials, although not too good for the health, look pedestrian when compared to work going on in England.

William Henry Fox Talbot originally used a silver chloride coating on paper to achieve his negative, but later tried a glass plate coated with egg white instead of the paper base. Collodion was then used to hold the light sensitive materials. In case this sounds innocuous, you should know that collodion is a solution of gun-cotton in ether. This adventure was called the wet-plate process.

You also need to know that Talbot eventually called his negatives 'calotypes' and they were the world's first permanent negatives. **Dr. Maddox** later eliminated the collodion by inventing a gelatine emulsion, thus creating the dry-plate process and permitting **George Eastman** to pioneer the celluloid roll film in 1889.

You may now appreciate why the death of the photographic heir in *Kind Hearts and Coronets* was taken so philosophically by the survivors — in all likelihood there were several such deaths weekly among the monied experimenters. A small bang in the darkroom, a few too many sniffs of mercury vapour, or an accidental ingestion of one or more of the other ingredients probably played hell with the population and may explain why they had to breed so assiduously, what with photography and the Empire to support.

There is no doubt about the interest in the subject. In the late 19th century housewives became acutely aware of a shortage of eggs, although chickens were laying normally and distribution was not being affected in any way. The explanation was simple. An article in the *Photographic Journal* gave a recipe for a new developer based upon the humble egg-white (albumen). Every dedicated amateur throughout the land dashed to his grocer for eggs. Fortunately the exercise proved to be both messy and unreliable, and photographers rapidly returned to tried and tested cheaper methods.

For the record, there was one potato based process, in 1904, the first practical colour emulsion, known as Autochrome and based on potato starch.

The most famous quote about the early processes comes from Paul Delaroche, the painter, whose reaction to the Daguerreotype was 'From today painting is dead' which with hindsight tells us more about his painting than about his prophecy.

FAMOUS NAMES

Photography is full of famous names. Personal names and product names abound and even the rankest amateur knows most of the manufacturers. So bluffers should have some names up their sleeves, which were attached to photographers, rather than products. This will put you ahead of most amateurs, who don't know them, and most professionals, who don't care about anyone except their role models and their direct competition.

The best way of getting maximum effect with minimum knowledge is to:

1. Preface your guess with a negative (so you get credit whether you are wrong or right)
2. Find a way of throwing in your second and third guesses (perhaps the only other two names you know).

For example, if you are faced with period monochrome photographs of exceedingly well-assembled young men, coyly facing away from the camera, with taut buttocks and interesting shadows, there is a strong possibility that **George Platt Lynes** was involved, one way or the other, but you cannot be certain. The correct line of attack could be "Surely that can't be an early Lynes? One sees so much of homo-erotica revived now — and not because it's out of copyright." You can then go on to muse "Of course it's unlikely to be **Bruce Weber** or **Robert Mapplethorpe**, whom he is believed to have influenced, because the period looks wrong, somehow." (The "somehow" is important because it enables you to be vague about your reason, if challenged.)

Armed with this technique it is safe to acquire a little knowledge about the more idiosyncratic photographers. As a group they are less exciting than the great eccentric painters and musicians and most have the normal complement of ears. None appears to have caused the death of their models while posing (like Lizzie Siddall, at the hands of Dante Gabriel Rossetti). There is no famous blind photographer to balance the deaf Beethoven. Even their love lives are not so notorious.

It will come as a relief to know that you do not need to know all the Victorians. There were a lot of them. Quotable names include **Matthew Brady**, the war photographer, who concentrated on the American Civil War and **Roger Fenton** who covered the Crimea. Their work is readily identified by the costumes coupled with the fact that there are absolutely no action shots — films and lenses were not up to it. You are more likely to have seen Brady's portraits, particularly the famous one of Abraham Lincoln, widely regarded as a crucial factor in the success of Lincoln's presidential campaign — perhaps the first instance of modern media interference in the democratic process.

Spare a thought too for **Alexander Gardner**, Brady's assistant, who was the first recorded sufferer from the filched picture problem still rife in professional circles.

Lewis Carroll is also quotable. Most people know he wrote *Alice in Wonderland* and was really the Reverend Charles Dodgson. Few people are aware that he specialised in pictures of little girls in coy poses and indeed coy outfits and gave up photography very suddenly. The charitable view is that this was due to his unwillingness to change from the wet collodion process to the newfangled dry plate.

Julia Cameron was a good example of the liberated though not emancipated Victorian lady. Hers is one of the few female names which survives from this period. The horrid darkroom processes mentioned earlier might have been a factor. Alternatively the hand and stand cameras which demanded good muscle tone and enlarged biceps rather than pectorals are more likely to have deterred women. You need to be aware that most of Mrs Cameron's sitters were the elite of the day and this is probably the reason for the survival of her products and hence her reputation. Professional photographers and bluffers may say her images left a lot to be desired.

Francis Frith was a photographer of record and we are never going to be allowed to forget it. Perhaps unfortunately for his memory a vast collection of his negatives has survived and is being marketed widely in every town and village which his early tours put on record. You would do him a service and enhance your own reputation by recalling his Egyptian temples rather than his English country scenes.

Eadweard Muybridge is the best known artist technician. He it was who first resolved the condundrum — what happens to a horse's legs when at the gallop. He was also credited with the murder of his wife's lover and his real name was Muggeridge.

Coming closer to the present it is not possible for the bluffer to remember all the photographers nor, with most of them is it possible to guess who took a specific photograph by its style. There are exceptions.

Man Ray is best known to photographers for his surreal effects and use of solarisation, which you can identify by the little halo effect round the edges of each change in tone. The effect may originally have been produced by accident because it demands that the material be whipped out of the soup during processing, given a brief and traumatic exposure to white light and then put back in again. One can assume that the first time it was accompanied by a expletive as the error was realised, followed by experiment as the result became apparent and tempted repetition. Nowadays technique is more outside the darkroom than in.

Dr. Harold Edgerton for example, the bête noir of available light photographers, in 1931 at MIT invented the flashgun (as distinct from the flash bulb) thereby taking photography even further from art in many eyes.

The main difficulty with all photographers is to recognise their work without spending hours staring at it. **Cartier Bresson** you will recall because his between-wars shot of the fat French family picnicking at the riverside has been so often reproduced. It is very characteristic of his work in that it is very French, very unposed, monochrome and preserved at what he calls the 'decisive moment' which, more than most of the above characteristics, may help you to identify his work. Not so the man himself who was seldom, if ever, photographed. This is allegedly so that his anonymity would be preserved to aid his future work. The bluffer may care to consider the alternative, which is that he had seen so much bad work from his contemporaries that he used his personal stature to protect himself from the ravages of amateur contemporaries.

Robert Capa also deserves a mention or two. He would be a contemporary photographer, had he not been killed in action. He is doomed to be remembered by one photograph, of the soldier in the Spanish Civil War, arms spread wide as he is (or perhaps, is not) shot. Now believed to have been posed, it is not necessary to prove this, just to know of the possibility. (The absence of blood is a pointer.) You could aid Capa's memory by quoting and emulating his advice: 'If your pictures aren't good enough, you aren't close enough'.

Theatre has many exponents. **Angus McBean** is probably *the* name here because he has done it so long, so well and is still doing it. However, **Lord Snowdon** also deserves an honourable mention for moving stage photography on from the posed and starchy prints which always looked younger than the Thespians pictured, to the modern style of press grab shots in available light. This is considerably more difficult than it looks. It also reminds you that he was at one point a competent and envied press photographer who helped to wean his colleagues from the heavy cameras of the postwar period to today's miniature and, of course, was photographer before peer, unlike **Lord Lichfield** who did it the other way round, but also on merit.

Another name whose work looks odd, was **Weegee**, whose candid photography in New York in the 1940s is instantly recognisable by its excessive contrast (very black, very white) and the faintly weird nature of his subjects. Even the normal looked odd in front of Weegee's lens and he had an eye for the oddity too. Useful because a few examples will permit authoritative later recognition of others. (Nobody else wanted results like this.)

Do make yourself aware of **Ralph Steadman**'s technique of distorting the soft emulsion of Polaroid prints just after they leave the camera, thereby make the subjects, frequently Tory politicians, look even more odd than they do in the flesh. This ensures that the *Observer* and the *Guardian* will print them. It is acceptable to hold an opinion about this work. Something simple will suffice, like "Awful by any standards". Conservative Central Office are believed to share this view.

Finally, here is a short list of some other recent and contemporary names the bluffer might be expected to know. Note that despite our earlier reservation about the lack of eccentricity, this includes a suicide, a Sherpa, a fraud, a government department as patron, and a nutter.

Ansel Adams

Both in musical and photographic circles it is useful to be able to mention that Ansel Adams trained as a concert pianist. This will impress people who only knew him for his landscapes. It will not actually impress the musical.

In an ideal world his landscapes would deter anyone from imitating him. Alas, the reverse applies, so any fool (except a bluffer) with a wide angle lens thinks he can emulate.

Diane Arbus

She moved from fashion to the ugly and eccentric. It is possible to refer to her as the Dorothy Parker of photography, not least because she took Parker's suicidal interest further, to implementation in 1971.

Bill Brandt

It is acceptable to describe Brandt as the greatest British photographer of the 20th century. His Russian descent probably helped.

David Bailey

You will have some difficulty finding general exhibitions with Bailey material. This is because he allegedly does not permit his work to be exhibited with others. A useful self-publicist, none the less.

Alfred Eisenstadt

It is not permissible to suggest that Eisenstadt invented the modern candid (not least because Cartier-Bresson, Kertesz and Salomon all did it first). Remember instead the VJ Day image of the young woman being thoroughly kissed in Times Square by a sailor — with her foot raised ecstatically behind her.

Farm Service Administration
The FSA sponsored a lot of superb photographers between the wars in rural America. Remember **Dorothea Lange** (their best), **Walker Evans**, **Russell Lee** and **Carl Mydans**.

Philippe Halomann
Whatever his merits, all you need to know is his obsession with 'jumpology' a theory that people show more of their inner selves (in their faces and attitudes) when aloft than when static. Fortunately this did not catch on.

Bert Hardy
The real talent behind *Picture Post* despite **Lorant**, **Hopkinson** and **Hulton**, who took most of the credit.

Yousuf Karsh
You will already know Karsh from his famous studio portrait of Churchill (the one where he achieved the bulldog expression by pinching Churchill's cigar a moment earlier). This is very typical of Karsh — impeccable technique, formal pose, studio based, famous sitter — which gives you a better chance of recognising his work than most.

Andre Kertesz
Kertesz is most easily remembered for his own comment that he did Leica work before Leitz invented the Leica. This (correctly) implies brilliant candid photojournalism. Born Hungarian, he became American.

Jacob Riis
Founder of photo-journalism. He changed the face of New York and early American towards the poor immigrant.

Gary Powers
Powers, of U2 fame, may not be the best aerial photographer or the most successful, but he is certainly the most famous, in part because of his lack of success. A useful name with which to trivialise the conversation.

Erich Salomon
Salomon was a diplomatic/political photographer. In the end he paid the equivalent of the war photographer's price and died in Auschwitz. Another brilliant candid reportage miniature worker.

Merlyn Severn
The female *Picture Post* great. Hardly known, perhaps because she wasn't male.

Susan Sontag
Produced one of the best books ever on photography — *On Photography*. It is a bluffer's dream too: no illustrations.

Laszlo Moholy-Nagy
Important for early photograms and later technical inventiveness. Remember just to prove you can pronounce correctly (last name rhymes with large).

Sabattier
The man who invented what everybody misdescribes as solarisation. It is not necessary to master the *real* technique, simply mention it.

Sherpa Tensing
A gentleman better known for his climbing skills, but his work has been more widely published than many well-known professionals. (Well, who do you think did all those shots of Hunt at the top of Mount Everest?)

GLOSSARY

As in other areas, photography has some unique words, and uses other ordinary words but with alternative meanings. Here are some you ought to know:

Aberration — That which adversely affects lens performance.

Adult, as in 'adult photographs' — Prurient appeal to juvenile minds.

Aperture — a) A hole, which in cameras is cunningly concealed inside the lens so that you have to peer through the lens to find it. b) The effective size of the hole as a measure of the light reaching the film. Relatively few amateurs know that the maximum aperture of the lens is actually the diameter of the hole, divided by the focal length of the lens. Reducing the size of the hole is known as **stopping down**.

Available light — Light that has not been enhanced by flash or flood. Photographers thus resort to making more available with reflectors, domestic lights, massed candles, etc. Called **existing light** in America — 'I bring it, therefore it exists'.

Backlight — When much or all of the light comes from behind the subject. Used to be called 'contre-jour'.

Bellows cameras — Acceptable generic term for any camera with a black pleated bag between lens and camera body.

Blowup — An enlargement, not anything military.

Blueprint — The result of a specialised document copying process. Nothing to do with photography, or saucy pictures.

Bracketing — The cautious process of taking several different exposures of the same subject, greater and lesser than the 'correct' setting in case your meter or guesswork is wrong.

Built-in, as in built in exposure meter — Included, but not coupled to the lens and shutter.

Candid photographs — Generic term for photographs taken without the subjects' knowledge and/or consent. No excuse for poor quality.

Circle of confusion — a) Professionals' view of an amateur gathering. b) The diameter of the largest out of focus area in a print which can be seen as a point at normal viewing distance.

Contact — Short form for 'contact print', a 1:1 print made in direct contact with the negative. Do not confuse with 'contact magazines' which introduce people with specialised sexual tastes to other people with identical or complementary needs.

Coupled — Linked, but not automatic.

Dedicated, as in dedicated flash — Feature that won't work with other cameras.

Definition — Indefinable precision.

Double exposure — When you are haunted by your ghost images.

ERC (Every Ready Case) — That which prevents you bringing the camera into action in less than 2.7 seconds.

Fast lenses — Those that admit a lot of light, and avoid the need for:

Fast films — Those that are grainier than slow ones.

Flair — What most amateurs lack. Professionals substitute technical competence and a lot of wasted film.

Flare — That which results from unplanned light.

Fixing — The process of making images permanent, nothing to do with drug abuse.

Glamour, as in glamour photography — Females without much or any of their clothing; frequently tasteless, never glamorous.

Graduate — Nothing to do with universities or Mrs Robinson, but a calibrated measure.

Grain — Visible fault that some photographers turn into a virtue.

Guide numbers — No help at all unless you know if it's based on feet or meters.

Incredible lens offer — Obsolete stock.

Instamatic — Neither instant nor automatic, but conveying a hint of both.

Leader — A fairly useless bit of film whose only reason for existence is that the useful and used bits of film have something to follow. It becomes useless (because exposed) before it can perform this function. Quite like other leaders, really.

Light fog — Patch caused by the intrusion of unwanted light.

Light tight — What a darkroom is until someone opens the door.

Light trap — Device which permits film but not light to pass through. Treat well or it scratches.

Mat, matt, matte — The surface finish of a photographic paper; the opposite of glossy. Something halfway between the two extremes is known as **lustre**, **semi-gloss** or **semi-matt**.

Mirror image — Any image which is reversed left to right. It confuses users who have to move the camera to the left to catch a subject vanishing off their screen to the right. Anyone waving a camera around like a windscreen wiper has not mastered this.

Macro lens — Any lens nowadays which can focus a bit closer than arm's length. (A true macro lens achieves 1.1 reproductions.)

Miniature camera — One that is slightly more pocketable.

Monochrome — One colour only, all shades of black.

Photofinishers — Commercial processors of film. Many terminate the product entrusted to their care, rather than just finish them.

Pull — Photojournalists' slang for exposing a film at a lower effective speed rating than that advised by the manufacturer, and compensating for it in later processing. Point out that the correct word for pull is **cut**, but the opposite is still to **push**.

RC paper — Resin coated paper, not *The Catholic Herald.*

Red-eye effect — Seeing red in a flash.

Resolution — The ability of a lens to resolve very fine subject detail on the film plane. Great if the film is up to it, fairly stupid if not, because you'll never see it.

Shot of a lifetime — One that didn't come out.

SLR — Single lens reflex.

TLR — Twin of the above.

Telephoto lens — Lens which is not as long, or even longer than, the focal length it claims.

Touching up — The secret need of most prints. It is safer to call it re-touching.

Reciprocity - As with any relationship, only mentioned when it fails.

THE AUTHOR

John Courtis has been playing with cameras for over forty years. He points out that he started very young. He now has over 25,000 negatives waiting to be catalogued, probably by his literary executors.

Photography has been therapy throughout his careers as accountant, consultant, editor, writer and headhunter.

Apart from the negatives and indeed the prints and slides, an astonishing array of over 100 cameras has passed through his hands including Agfa, Beirette, Canon, Corfield, Dekko, Exacta, Foth, Gilbert, Houghton, Ilford, K.W., Konica, Leica, Minox, Minolta, Olympus, Pentax, Ricoh, Rollei, Swinger, Topcon, Voigtländer, Wirgin, Yashica, Zenit, Zorki and Zeiss.

He writes from personal experience of nearly all the things bluffers are advised to avoid (and is seriously trying to give them up).

THE BLUFFER'S GUIDES

Available now @ £1.00 each:

Accountancy
Antiques
Bluffing
Class
Computers
Consultancy
Feminism
Golf
Hi-Fi
Hollywood
Jazz
Literature

Management
Marketing
Music
Paris
Philosophy
Photography
Publishing
Sex
Teaching
Television
Theatre
Wine

Coming March 1988:

Ballet
Cricket
Maths

All these books are available at your local bookshop or newsagent, or can be ordered direct from the publisher. Just tick the titles you require and fill in the form below. Prices and availability subject to change without notice.

Ravette Limited, 3 Glenside Estate, Star Road, Partridge Green, Horsham, West Sussex RH13 8RA

Please send a cheque or postal order, and allow the following for postage and packing. UK 25p for one book and 10p for each additional book ordered.

Name ....

Address...

....

THE BLUFFER'S GUIDES

In preparation:

Advertising
Architecture
Astrology
Bank Managers
Beliefs
The Body
Cinema
The Classics
Defence
Espionage
Finance
Gambling
High Society
Journalism
Law
Millionaires
Modern Art
Opera
Politics
Property
Psychiatry

Public Relations
Secret Societies
Selling
Ski-ing
Stocks & Shares
Travel
University
World Affairs

The Americans
The Australians
The British
The French
The Germans
The Japanese

Amsterdam
Berlin
Hong Kong
Moscow
New York